Christopher Comma

Written by Barbara Cooper
Illustrated by Maggie Raynor

GARETH STEVENS
GS
PUBLISHING
A Member of the WRC Media Family of Companies

Please visit our web site at: www.garethstevens.com
For a free color catalog describing our list of high-quality books,
call 1-800-542-2595 (USA) or 1-800-387-3178 (Canada).

Library of Congress Cataloging-in-Publication Data

Cooper, Barbara, 1929-
   [Colin Comma]
   Christopher Comma / written by Barbara Cooper; illustrated by Maggie
Raynor. — North American ed.
      p. cm. — (Meet the Puncs: A remarkable punctuation family)
      Summary: Introduces the use of the comma through the story of Christopher,
a member of the Punc family who is always cheerful and loves to sing.
      ISBN-10: 0-8368-4224-3 (lib. bdg.)
      ISBN-13: 978-0-8368-4224-1 (lib. bdg.)
      [1. Comma—Fiction.   2. English language—Punctuation—Fiction.]
   I. Raynor, Maggie, 1946- , ill. II. Title.
   PZ7.C78467Ch   2004
   [E]—dc22   2004045217

This edition first published in 2005 by
Gareth Stevens Publishing
A Weekly Reader© company
1 Reader's Digest Road
Pleasantville, NY 10570-7000 USA

This U.S. edition copyright © 2005 by Gareth Stevens, Inc. Original edition
copyright © 2003 by Compass Books Ltd., UK. First published in 2003 as
(The Puncs) an adventure in punctuation: Colin Comma by Compass Books Ltd.

Designed and produced by Allegra Publishing Ltd., London
Gareth Stevens editor: Dorothy L. Gibbs
Gareth Stevens art direction: Tammy West

Printed in the United States of America

3 4 5 6 7 8 9 10 09 08 07

Christopher Comma,

who is called Chris,
is the busiest,
happiest,
and most
cheerful
of the Puncs,

Hi, all.

and he
loves
to sing.

3

In the mornings, from seven o'clock until noon, Chris delivers the mail.

In the afternoons, from two o'clock until three o'clock, he washes windows,

and, in the evenings,
from seven o'clock
until nine o'clock,

he delivers fresh fruits,
vegetables, and eggs.

Chris lives with his wife, Carrie, and their two children, Carl and Chloe, at Comma Cottage, Punc Lane, Commaville, which is a village near Commaford, not far from Commatown.

When Chris was a small boy, his mother, Catherine, who is called Cathy, noticed that he had a sweet, clear singing voice, which is not surprising because his father, Carter, sings in a male chorus, and he often performs solos in his deep, bass voice.

Just after Chris reached the age of six, Cathy decided that it was time he had singing lessons, so she took him to see Mr. Punctone, who is the organist at the local church, and who could tell, after listening to only a few notes, that Chris could carry a tune.

do, re, mi, fa...

howl, howl

Chris became a star member of the church choir, singing show tunes, folk songs, country ballads, etc., and he also taught himself to play the guitar and, later, joined a pop music group, which was called the Rolling Puncs.

Next to singing, Chris loves being outdoors, and he loves chatting with people, which is why he decided to be a mail carrier.

When he is on his rounds, pushing his mail cart, Chris often bursts into song. Generally, however, because of the traffic, no one can hear him!

As a mail carrier, Chris enjoys delivering the postcards, letters, packages, and parcels that make people happy,

but he hates junk mail.

"What a waste of paper, wood, and trees," he grumbles, sorting through pamphlets, leaflets, flyers, circulars, samples, and so on.

After lunch every day, Chris cleans windows. He loads his van with equipment, including his ladder, his bucket, his chamois, and his squeegee, then he sets off for the houses of his regular customers, who are the same people as on his mail route.

Of course, believe it or not, Chris sings as he works!

19

Chris likes to be on the move, morning, noon, and night. After he finishes cleaning windows, he jumps into his van, drives to the little farm down the lane, and starts work again, picking up boxes of fruits, vegetables, and eggs and loading them into his van.

Sometimes, on summer evenings, but not after dark, Chris's children, Chloe, age nine, and Carl, age seven, help Chris deliver the fruits, vegetables, and eggs, wheeling them to customers' doors in an old baby carriage.

Also, during the summer, Chris, Carrie, Chloe, and Carl spend a lot of time going for long walks. Because they are concerned about conservation, they are careful to stay on the paths, obey the signs, close gates behind them, pick up litter, and, in general, look after the countryside.

Now and then, the Comma family packs up the van, for a vacation, and goes to visit Chris's cousins, Calvin and Colin, who live in Comma Center, near Puncton.

Occasionally, Chris takes his guitar, Calvin takes his banjo, and Colin takes his fiddle, and off they go, for an evening out, to entertain customers at a local club, playing and singing their favorite songs.

Chris gets along with all of the other Puncs, except Peter Period.

While Peter is trying to do his job, which is to make things stop, Chris keeps getting in the way, pushing his mail cart, putting up his ladder, parking his van, walking along country lanes, always on the move, never, ever, stopping!

So, by now, you should see that

Christopher Comma, besides being cheerful, kind, helpful, energetic, and always singing, is so busy that he never knows when to stop, and, although he is very useful for breaking up long sentences, like this one, he is unable, no matter how hard he tries, to bring them to an end, forcing Peter Period to come to the rescue, like this ●

Christopher's Checklist

- Use commas to separate items that are listed in a series:
  Chris sorts through pamphlets, leaflets, flyers, circulars, samples, and so on.

- Use commas to separate two or more describing words (adjectives):
  Chris is the busiest, happiest, and most cheerful of the Puncs.

- Use a comma to write dates:
  January 21, 2003

- Use a comma to separate two parts of a sentence when one part begins with a connecting word such as *when*, *although*, *if*, *because*, *who*, or *which*:
  When Chris was a small boy, his mother noticed that he had a good singing voice.

- Use a pair of commas to separate a fact or explanation from the rest of a sentence:
  In the mornings, from seven o'clock until noon, Chris delivers the mail.

- A comma can also separate a fact from a question:
  Chris is a busy Punc, isn't he?

- Introductory words, such as *well*, *now*, *sometimes*, *today*, or *yes*, are followed by a comma:
  Sometimes, Chloe and Carl help Chris make deliveries.

- Use a comma to separate two sentences joined together with a linking word (conjunction) such as *and*, *but*, or *so*:
  Chris enjoys delivering letters, but he hates junk mail.

- Use commas to introduce, interrupt, or end quotations:
  Chris said, "I love to sing."
  "I'm busy," said Chris, "but I will deliver your eggs later."
  "What a waste of trees," he said.

- Use a comma to help make sentences clear:
  To Chris, using commas makes perfect sense.

- Use a comma to write numbers in the thousands:
  1,000 2,000 3,000

- Commas are used to break up parts of an address and other kinds of instructions:
  Comma Cottage, Punc Lane, Commaville, Puncland